It's *All* About *Love* in Relationships

It's All About Love in Relationships

A Guide for Single People
Preparing for the Right Mate

Tiffany Louise Wade

LOWBAR
PUBLISHING COMPANY

905 South Douglas Avenue • Nashville, Tennessee 37204
Phone: 615-972-2842
E-mail: Lowbarpublishingcompany@gmail.com
Web site: www.Lowbarbookstore.com

Copyright © 2017 Tiffany Louise Wade

No part of this book may be reproduced or transmitted in any form or by any means—graphic, electronic, or mechanical, including photocopying, recording, taping, or by any information storage retrieval system—without the permission, in writing, of the publisher or author.

Lowbar Publishing Company
905 S. Douglas Ave.
Nashville, Tennessee 37204
615-972-2842
Lowbarpublishingcompany@gmail.com
www.Lowbarbookstore.com

Editor: Honey B. Higgins
Graphic and Cover Design Artist: Norah S. Branch

Unless otherwise noted, Scripture references in this book are taken from the King James Version of the Holy Bible.

Printed in the United States of America.
ISBN: 978-0-9969432-4-6

For additional information or to contact the author for workshops or seminars, please call 615-478-8160, or e-mail t_wade07@yahoo.com or Lowbarpublishingcompany@gmail.com.

www.facebook.com/thetiffanywade

This book is dedicated to all those who desire to have a spouse, and who believe that God has already answered their prayer. I also dedicate this book to my youth organization, Building Youth Partnerships. I pray that the youth and young adults will take heed to the advice in this book when they begin to date. The youth are the future. It is our duty to train them, and to show a positive example of good leadership.

Table of Contents

Foreword 9

Introduction 11

Chapter

   1   Looking for Mr. Right or Mrs. Right 13

   2   No FWBs (Friends with Benefits) 22

   3   Summertime Fine 32

   4   Old-school Love 41

   5   You're the One..51

Poem: God Is All About Love 62

About the Author...63

Foreword

We are once again thankful to God for allowing our daughter, Tiffany L. Wade, to write her second book, *It's All About Love in Relationships: A Guide for Single People Preparing for the Right Mate*. Moreover, it amazes us to see how hard she works, and the time she has dedicated to write each book thus far.

This book will challenge some single people to assert godly wisdom and knowledge in their relationships. After all, relationships can sometimes be complex and difficult to handle without God. Also, as you read, you will learn some great key testimonies from other relationships.

We find this book to be an easy guide on how to experience God's love and how to seek to build a godly relationship before marriage, so that your marriage can be blessed by God. Moreover, as you read, we hope that the Scriptures will sanctify your heart forever, fill your heart with love, and encourage you to look (watch) and wait until God sends you the right mate.

God bless!

Drs. Louis and Betty Wade

Introduction

Relationships have been around since the beginning of time. When God created Adam and saw that Adam was alone, He created Eve to be his helpmate. This book was inspired by the Holy Spirit, and the advice given is for single people who are looking to get married one day. Marriage is a gift from God, and a very precious covenant. God created marriage for His glory, and He wants us to keep Him first, even in our marriages. Those seeking to get married need to know that lust, adultery, and pride are huge downfalls in marriage. I believe that what you cannot control in your life as a single person will become a pattern in your married life; so if lust and engaging in sex with multiple partners are things that control you, then now is the time to change it—while you are single.

This book will help you realize what precautions to take while dating, and how to prepare yourself for marriage. Many people want someone who is the "total package," knowing that they themselves are far from being the total package. You can look for Mr. Right or Mrs. Right all day, but if you are not equally yoked in Christ with your significant other, then you are missing out on an opportunity to have a godly relationship. God wants all of us to have a blessed life—but to live a blessed life, you have to stay in the will of God. While reading this book, I hope that you change your way of thinking about relationships, and that you will be more mindful of the people you attract and entertain. Relationships are the most important part of life. This book will also give you key components to help you navigate this world, and be better prepared for dating and marriage. If you remember nothing else, please remember to keep God first in your relationship. He should be the Head of your life, and in everything you do acknowledge Him (see Proverbs 3:6). I must note that the title of each chapter of this book stems from the titles of my songs from my EP "It's All About Love."

My aunt, Evangelist Ellen Harris-Harvey (Radio Host for Spiritual Connections Outreach Ministry, Inc), and myself

CHAPTER 1

Looking for Mr. Right or Mrs. Right

Looking for Mr. Right or Mrs. Right is always a main topic of conversation throughout the world today. When you log onto your social media accounts, I can guarantee that you will see someone posting something pertaining to relationships and the woes of being single. We live in a society where people are always looking for love and "the right one." I can remember how, while in college, my friends and I always talked about one day getting married, having a beautiful family, and having great careers. As a matter of fact, one time my best friend and I went to a jewelry store to look at engagement rings. We were looking for rings to get ideas of the type of ring we would like to have when we marry "Mr. Right." However, years later I have become more aware of the societal stigma that is on relationships, love, and marriage. Believe it or not, our generation (the Millennials) still believe in relationships, love, and marriage, but we like to take our time. There are many women in the world looking for Mr. Right, and trying to fit into the societal norm of being the "One" for a man that doesn't even know who he is.

From my own past experiences, I have noticed how easy it is to get caught up in wanting to be in a relationship and having someone to love you. When I was in college, I dated in hopes of finding Mr. Right, and I later realized that I had to find myself. There are so many people getting married, and they do not even know much about themselves, or they don't know what their purpose in life is. There is nothing wrong with looking for the right person, but don't allow that to deter you away from discovering your purpose in life. Furthermore, many women like myself, who are traditional when it comes to dating, believe that Mr. Right will find you. The Bible illustrates, "Whoso findeth a wife findeth a good thing, and obtaineth favour of the LORD" (Proverbs 18:22).

Let's get to the nitty-gritty of looking for "Mr. Right." Here is a scenario that, in most cases, happens with women today: A young woman goes to the club every weekend wearing the hottest outfit, and gets hit on by every guy she walks past. She collects several numbers every weekend, and guys even message her online. She goes on dates at least once or twice a week with different guys. However, she is still lonely and has a void in her heart. She is on the prowl and looking high and low for the right guy, but she has yet to find him. Nevertheless, she is like many women who are out there looking for Mr. Right yet keep running into a dead end. If you are this person, ask yourself, "Why am I looking? Am I content with who I am? Do I know my purpose in life?" If you don't know the answers to these questions, then maybe it is time to evaluate yourself, and stop looking for someone to fill a void which only God can fill. If you are not whole as a person, then you have no idea what Mr. Right or Mrs. Right looks like.

There are so many people that can dress up like the right person for you, but who are not right for you. You see, God has an appointed time for everything in your life. He knows who He has for you, but when you are ready. And you will not find it a moment earlier. Furthermore, we spend so much time looking that we don't realize that as soon as we stop looking, what we are looking for is right in front of us. It's like when you are looking for shoes you stored away for the summer and cannot find them—until you stop looking and that is when they appear. However, as a single person it is best to prepare for what you want. The best way to prepare for anything is to pray, meditate, and allow God to guide you. Spend your time as a single person being productive and learning new things about yourself. Do not be the person always using his/her time looking for Mr. Right or Mrs. Right, because once you get married those single years are over. If you go around and ask a few married couples right now, I'm sure that most of them would tell you to embrace your singleness. To be honest, from my own experience as a single person, I have been able to accomplish some amazing projects that I did not believe I would have been able to accomplish had I not been single. God wants the same for you!

He created us all with a purpose—to do His will—and the gifts He has given us are just small aspects to help us do what we're supposed to do. Those gifts He gave you can only be fully developed when you know who you are in Christ, and what your purpose is on earth. The only way you can know your life's purpose is for you to spend time with God as a single person. God must shape and mold you, and lead you to be the person He created you to be. According to research, the reason why divorce rates are so high is because a person may jump into marriage without being complete as an individual. You cannot expect someone else to complete you, and you cannot expect someone to complement you if you are not complete in Christ. People tend to look for others to fill a void brought on by hurt, rejection, and insecurity. However, your looking for someone to complete you will only break your heart more. I have learned from past experiences that you must put your trust in the Lord.

> **Trust in the LORD with all thine heart; and lean not unto thine own understanding. In all thy ways acknowledge him, and he shall direct thy paths.** (Proverbs 3:5-6)

When you completely trust God, you will be able to sleep peacefully and enjoy life, whether you have Mr. Right/Mrs. Right or not.

Patience is another key component. With anything in life, you must learn how to wait. So, why not wait for the right person, one sent by God to be united with in marriage? It is no different from waiting on the right opportunity to take off in your career. When you have worked so hard and been patient, good will come to you. Wait on the Lord to show you the right person in His appointed time.

> **The LORD is good unto them that wait for him, to the soul that seeketh him.** (Lamentations 3:25)

Everyone has a season of being single, so why not spend your season of being single doing what you love, and having a fun time with your family and friends? Seasons are temporary; even when you look at nature, you notice that autumn comes after summer. You cannot skip seasons because you want all your blessings instantly. If God gave you everything you wanted or prayed for all at once, you could not handle it. Each season you go through allows you to mature and blossom into a better person. Jumping from relationship to relationship does not give you a chance to go through the healing and restoration season; instead, you continue to stay stagnant in the season that you are not supposed to dwell in. I say that to catch Mr. Right or Mrs. Right you have to be available (Hello, somebody)! You are clearly unavailable when you jump in and out of relationships. Many times, women think that they can turn a man into Mr. Right because he seems to have potential. Needless to say, never fall in love with potential, because God wants you to have the best! You can't expect the best when you are not at your best. Moreover, take time to learn, be healthy, and be actively involved with the community. Spend your single days helping other people, so you don't get caught up in looking for love in the wrong places. The busier you become in your purpose, the more likely you are going to meet Mr. Right or Mrs. Right!

In light of that, marriage was created for a purpose; God ordained it for two people to serve a purpose together. So, when you find your purpose, and you are walking in your purpose, it's safe to say that you will meet your match. God has a purpose for all of us, and once you take a chance to follow the Holy Spirit, you will get to your destination. One thing I have learned is that no one can stop destiny. If it is meant for you to meet Mr. Right or Mrs. Right tomorrow, or next week, it will happen. There will be challenges you face, but destiny will always win. I see people always posting on Facebook that they are lonely or tired of dating, and so on, but the best advice I can give is to wait and hear from God regarding who you should date. What is meant to be will be. However, I am not saying that you should not date at all, but be selective, and learn some things about the person you are dating. Patience is a must when it comes to dating, because you will save yourself a lot of time away from heartbreak and abuse.

Furthermore, it is never a good idea to pour out your heart to someone you don't know; many times doing so can easily turn someone off. You may be dating your Mr. Right or Mrs. Right at this moment, but please take your time and allow nature to take its course. Moving too fast can be detrimental to any relationship, and can be a huge spoiler alert. It is better to know a person as a friend first, and share with each other as friends, so you can have a solid friendship. A marriage without a solid friendship will be a disaster. When you and your mate have a great friendship, there is very little that could tear you apart. You will know that the grass is not necessarily greener on the other side. Not to mention, you realize that no one is perfect and that you can't judge or hold grudges against your significant other. In addition, when you are friends with each other first you can share your life with your mate and gain a better understanding of your mate. Mr. Right or Mrs. Right should be your best friend—that is the only way it is going to last and work for both parties' benefit.

Most importantly, when looking for Mr. Right or Mrs. Right, you should assess what your relationship with God is like. Do you put God first, or are you so caught up in being with someone that you forget about God? Maybe God is leading you closer to Him for a reason, so that you can live your life as a whole person. Without God, you cannot function, and you cannot make it to the point of success that you were created to reach. I've seen so many people live their lives chasing "booty" that they completely missed their time of true success. It is really sad to see people go through life chasing what is not for them. God wants your heart first! Stop giving it up to people that do not mean you any good! No one in this world could love you more than God does, and He will send you the right person to love you here on earth in the right season.

But seek ye first the kingdom of God, and his righteousness; and all these things shall be added unto you. (Matthew 6:33)

When you seek God first and walk in His will, greatness is there for you! Your seeking ungodly love in this world will leave you lonely and worried. And, life without God will leave you dried up like a prune. In my lifetime, I have noticed many people in their forties who look like they are in their sixties because they aren't satisfied with who they are, and don't know their purpose in life. You must find your purpose and seek God first. When you both walk in purpose as individuals, and you come together, imagine how powerful your lives will be as one!

Therefore shall a man leave his father and his mother, and shall cleave unto his wife: and they shall be one flesh. (Genesis 2:24)

Being single gives you that time to develop and tap into that God-given power you were born with. Use your single time to your advantage! I thank God that He is allowing me to have this time of being single, and to not feel the need to jump into something that may end up being detrimental to my purpose. If Mr. Right or Mrs. Right is not helping you with your purpose and bringing out the best in you, then it is best to move forward and complete your journey as an individual. Your God-given mate will bring out the best parts of you, and help you with the parts you struggle with. God knows what you need, and when you need it.

Sometimes, we look for the right mate everywhere we think he/she may be, not noticing that God has already placed the right person in our lives. We are so busy wanting to subscribe to the world's standard of Mr. Right or Mrs. Right that we overlook what God has for us. Oftentimes we get so impatient and we settle for whatever, because we don't want to wait. When I was in college, I dated a guy that I wanted so badly to be in a relationship with, but God showed me that I needed to wait, and I am glad that I did. If it were left up to me, I would have been married to that guy by now, yet God did not allow that to happen because He knows the bigger picture.

If you knew what God has in store for you, you wouldn't choose to settle. That is why it is good to be selective. I believe it is good to write down qualities and personality traits you want your mate to possess, such as being a Christian, respectful, kind, secure, etc. Those traits are way more important than physical features, because looks and beauty will fade. You have to connect with someone spiritually and mentally, because that will bring you closer together with your mate intimately. There is nothing worse than being with someone you can't be open or honest with. Honesty is very important in any relationship, even friendships. I know we live in a society where people tend to cover up who they really are and their past mistakes, but when you can be honest with someone, that goes very far.

I know that while dating, many people run into those types who don't want to commit, or don't want anything serious. It is sad that our society has become so comfortable with not committing; decades ago, the normal thing to do was commit. Our generation (Millennials) like to test drive everything, even going so far as to lease with an option to buy. My question has always been, why doesn't our generation like to commit? Is it because we have been so comfortable with just being friends and having more options, or is it because of fear? From what I have noticed, it could be both.

We have strayed away from the right way to date, and it has taken a toll on people mentally and spiritually. Every day, people hold conversations on the concept of being "friends with benefits"; this is so because, deep down, they know that this is not a good type of relationship to be in. When looking for Mr. Right or Mrs. Right, you should not settle for being "just friends"—tell potential love interests that no "friends with benefits" is allowed.

The next chapter is dedicated to the subject of being "friends with benefits." It's about to get real!

CHAPTER 2

No FWBs (Friends with Benefits)

Being "friends with benefits" is a way that people get sex, dates, or money without committing. Society has adapted to this way of thinking when it comes to relationships, to the point that marriage is not a goal. By the way, most relationship goals today measure the amount of people that one has sex with and deceives. I learned that some men and women like to have many options, and they like to sleep with whomever they can get. It is great to have options, but it is wise to be selective in dating; you should not have sex with everyone that comes along, because it can lead to sexually transmitted diseases and unwanted pregnancies. I believe that the concept of "friends with benefits" is a form of greed, because someone is getting everything he or she wants from several different people without committing to an exclusive relationship.

DON'T BE GREEDY! HIV and AIDS are no joke, and there are many people who have the disease that don't even know it. Furthermore, there are people who do have HIV or AIDS that know it, and they purposely sleep with people to infect them. Be selective, and tell people that you don't believe in being "friends with benefits," and, if they don't respond right, respectfully move on. When you move on, you will be glad that you did not connect yourself to someone that does not want to commit to a monogamous relationship.

I was taught that sex is supposed to be set aside for marriage, because sex can be a gateway to someone's soul. When you connect yourself with someone sexually you are connecting yourself with that person spiritually as well. Anytime you have sex with someone, you are connecting yourself to that person. And, many people who jump into the "friends with benefits" situation together don't really know each other well, and when they have sex, everything changes and becomes unstable. I believe that having sex before being committed is not a good idea; it will always leave you empty and confused. There is a reason why God does not want us to be unequally yoked with others. Everything God says is for a reason.

Be ye not unequally yoked together with unbelievers: for what fellowship hath righteousness with unrighteousness? and what communion hath light with darkness? (2 Corinthians 6:14)

Having sex before marriage can lead to your experiencing a bad soul tie (spirit) between you and the person you've slept with, especially when you and the other person are unequally yoked. The devil and his demons use sex as a gateway to enter people, and they will have them riding an emotional roller coaster. From what I have noticed, people who have several sex partners go through a lot of emotional stability problems, because they've had too many soul ties with unstable people. Your having a sexual soul tie with someone who has an ungodly motive can cause so many things to go sour in your life, and can cause you to miss out on so many blessings. People don't realize that sex is like a drug, and allowing someone to have sex with you without a commitment can be a hard thing to get away from. Some "friends with benefits" situations can last for years, because of the participants' addiction to the sex. The best way to overcome this scenario is to not allow it to happen in the first place. However, for those who are in this situation, the best thing you can do is pray and take action, and cease entertaining someone who doesn't want to commit to you. Opening Pandora's box allows temptation to creep in, and it can be hard to resist. God wants us to flee from temptation and not get distracted by it.

Blessed is the man that endureth temptation: for when he is tried, he shall receive the crown of life, which the Lord hath promised to them that love him. (James 1:12)

When you endure temptation and don't fall into the traps the devil has set for you, God will bless you. The "friends with benefits" situation is a trap, because there is no honor in giving yourself to someone who doesn't respect you enough to commit. A real man or woman will commit and put a ring on it! They will show you how much they care for you. Not to mention the fact that I have seen so many people get hurt by playing the role of a wife or husband without a ring to the point that they take a lot of bitterness into their next relationship. These situations usually end with neither party experiencing anything but brokenness. Having sex with someone you have not committed to may feel good in the moment, but after the peak of the experience, you're right back to reality. I cannot understand how people like being on an emotional roller coaster, only to have the ride lead to that feeling of brokenness.

Another reason why some people prefer having a "friends with benefits" type of relationship is because of money.

For the love of money is the root of all evil: which while some coveted after, they have erred from the faith, and pierced themselves through with many sorrows. (1 Timothy 6:10)

The love of money has been one of the main portals the devil has used to tempt people since the beginning of time. It's surprising what people will do for money. There are even dating sites for people to hook up with people, just for money. Some women use men, under the premise of having a "friends with benefits" relationship, just to get those men to pay their bills and buy them things. In return, the man usually wants sexual benefits, and both individuals end up using each other for favors. To tell the truth, deep down inside people don't like being used and abused, whether it be for money or for sex. Many times, when someone has a lot of money, especially a man, temptation will come from every direction. As hard as it is for men to commit, money and power's being in the mix makes it easier to fall into the trap of being in a "friends with benefits" relationship.

Surprisingly, there are many women who are down to be with a man that will not commit to them just so they can be taken care of financially. Sadly, love is not even in the equation anymore. Instead of a relationship being "all about love," it's all about benefits. Why not benefit from godly love, trust, loyalty, and intimacy? When you are strong enough not to fall into the "friends with benefits" category, you will reap the best benefits. Find your purpose in Christ, and don't date beneath your purpose. In all honesty, you should be committed to someone who has a similar background and morals as you have. Never settle for anything less than what God has for you! Furthermore, don't use people and become known as the girl or guy that has "been around," because I have noticed that those types of people end up old and alone, or they have to settle for less. Attract what you want, and never lower your standards because of other people's opinions. Believe that God has the best for you, and that no weapon formed against you will prosper. Most importantly, carry yourself with class and integrity. When you carry yourself with class, people will respect you more, and your relationships will last.

    Relationships should always be about love, not just "love" in the sense of always benefitting from what the other person has to offer materially. And even when a friendship isn't a sexual one, there is no excuse for trying to benefit from someone's kindness in other ways, to the extent of using him or her for ulterior motives. If God's love isn't in the equation, then what is the point of that friendship or being in a relationship? We will always benefit from a relationship that is based in the love of Christ. When we don't feel like we are obligated to do this or that, we will do things for people simply out of love.

    Let all your things be done with charity.
(1 Corinthians 16:14)

    The love of God is always the key to life. There is a reason why God wants us to do all things out of love. When you do things out of love, there will be an everlasting impact on people's lives. People never forget when someone has helped them from a place of love and not just to reap benefits. Everything Jesus did here on this earth was done out of love. The way He operated in all aspects of His life changed the course of history, and has been an example of how to love unconditionally. Jesus is all about love, and His life was sacrificed so that we could have everlasting life and love others. Love does not waver or hurt—it is patient and kind (see 1 Corinthians 13:4-7). True love has no strings attached. Chasing a "friends with benefits" relationship can result in loneliness, anger, and bitterness. Yet, when you are patient and wait on true love, you will benefit in more than one way. God created us to function in body, soul, and spirit, just as He functions as God the Father, Son, and Holy Spirit. In order for us to function the best, we have to be whole—and in order for us to be whole, we have to have body, soul, and spirit on the same frequency. Your being in a "friends with benefits" relationship will cause you to be out of sync. As I stated before, when you have sex with someone to whom you are not married, one of those three things will be out of sync, and you could possibly become emotionally unstable.

It is true that some people equate lust with love—but lust is not love. Lust is a temporary feeling of infatuation and gives people a delusional perception of what love is *not*. According to the American Psychological Association, 40 to 50 percent of marriages end in divorce, and the main reasons behind that are lust and money. So many people get married for reasons concerning lust, and by the time they realize it, they've already signed the divorce papers. It is even worse when children are involved, because they suffer from their parents' wrong decisions. Lust and infatuation can be very destructive for families; they have caused so many families to separate. Lust is something you must flee from.

Flee also youthful lusts: but follow righteousness, faith, charity, peace, with them that call on the Lord out of a pure heart. (2 Timothy 2:22)

I know that fleeing from "youthful lust" is hard, because this world is full of lust. It seems like right around every corner, lust is right there looking you straight in your face. Lust is another gateway that the devil uses to lure people away from God and their purpose. Chasing "friends with benefits" relationships is a way that lust is put into action. And once lust is put into action, spiritual warfare starts. We all engage in spiritual warfare daily, but that is no reason for us to put ourselves in something destructive and on a roller coaster ride of emotions. Needless to say, we tend to love challenges, with many people settling for the "friends with benefits" relationship in hopes of changing the other person's mind. What these people tend to find, however, is that six months to a year later the other person still has not changed his/her mind.

Stop settling for that! Don't allow people to use you and take advantage of you. Again, God wants the best for all of us—I can't say that enough. I reiterate that, speaking from experience, it is wise for you to wait for the right person and not lower your standards for someone who is not for you. Once you settle for that person, it may be hard for you to reach your full potential. The decision regarding who you choose to marry has a huge impact on your life's journey. Settling for a lustful relationship can take your attention away from what God has called you to do. Take a moment to think about how much energy and time you may have wasted on a "friends with benefits" relationship. Those relationships can be so poisonous that, sometimes, it can take years for a person to get back on track. Remember that time wasted cannot be retrieved.

I do hope, however, that a lesson was learned during that moment in your life. God allows things to happen for a reason, and what you learn will always help you in the future. And the goal is that once you learn a lesson, you should try not to repeat the same mistake over and over again. For example, you may date the same type of person, or habitually get back into an unhealthy relationship after you've been mistreated or abused. You need to stop trying to make something work that isn't good for you. This may sound cliché, but some people are only around for a season, so stop giving seasonal people lifetime benefits. As a matter of fact, I had to go through some of my own experiences to learn that some relationships are not meant to last, which goes for friendships as well. Not everyone around you has good intentions, and usually you will know this in the beginning, if you watch a person's actions. People who want a "friends with benefits" relationship are flat-out using that situation to get what they want without committing to someone else. Once you figure out a person's intentions, move on, and never look back.

And Jesus said unto him, No man, having put his hand to the plough, and looking back, is fit for the kingdom of God. (Luke 9:62)

Not looking back is the best thing you can do. When you move on and stay focused, success will come your way. On the other hand, when you keep looking back, you can easily slip into depression or bitterness. Also, it can be hard to reach your goals when you are constantly bringing up the past or going back to that broken relationship. Instead, you want a relationship that benefits you spiritually, physically, and mentally. Nevertheless, when you wait, God will send you the right mate, who will help you meet your goals and help you grow spiritually. When a relationship is always confusing and filled with drama, that is a clear sign that the relationship is not fit for you. Move on and let it go. Tell the person you will not settle for being "friends with benefits"! Doing this shows that you have standards.

Having standards is very important—it will not only attract the right mate, but it will also help you maintain a healthy relationship with your mate. I don't know anyone who doesn't want a long-term, committed, and healthy relationship in life. The key to longevity in a relationship is to put God first and wait for Him to send His best. God wants you to trust and depend on Him for what you need. When you put God first, no good thing will He withhold from you. For example, as a parent you would want your child to have the best of everything. Furthermore, as a parent you know when your child is ready for certain things, so you make your child wait until the time is right. Thus, it is the same with God: He knows what's best for you, and He will have you to wait until the time is right to receive it. The best relationship to have is one with God, which will give you the strength not to settle for less. With God, you will have peace and joy within your relationship, and when the tough times come, your relationship will stand the test.

      A good relationship is built on a solid foundation, not a "friends with benefits" foundation. To put it in other words, those relationships are temporary, and you can't expect a relationship to last that was doomed to fail from the beginning. You have to learn to keep moving and realize that you don't have to continue to make those same mistakes. Do something different this time; raise your standards and stick with them. If you want a different result, do something different, and I guarantee that the next relationship will be completely different. Plus, once you raise your standards, certain people will not stay around long—and that is a good thing. If someone can't wait for you and respect you, then it is best to let that person walk away, because he or she is more of a liability in your life than an asset. An asset is valuable, but a liability is not—it can drain you in more than one way. Yet, many people continue to let liabilities grow in their lives, because they keep making the same mistake over and over again. They are afraid to let go because of fear. Some people are afraid to be alone or ridiculed because they are thirty-five or older and still single. But, loneliness is temporary, and it is nothing to be afraid of. When you have Jesus, you are never alone.

> **Teaching them to observe all things whatsoever I have commanded you: and, lo, I am with you always, even unto the end of the world. Amen.**
> (Matthew 28:20)

Most importantly, age is never anything to fear, because God knows when the time is right for you. Not everyone gets married by age 25 or 30, and that is okay. Even if you're 35 or older and still single, remember that God is preparing the best for you. As soon as you stop settling for "Netflix and chill" moments, you will have the best moments of your life. You have not begun to see all the great things that God has set for your future. The best is yet to come.

So the Lord blessed the latter end of Job more than his beginning: for he had fourteen thousand sheep, and six thousand camels, and a thousand yoke of oxen, and a thousand she asses. (Job 42:12)

Just like God blessed Job, He will bless you. Whenever God allows things to fall apart in your life, remember that He is working on your behalf, and He will give you double for your trouble. He loves you more than anyone could love you on this earth. He is preparing you for the best life you could ever have. Continue to be patient and trust that God is working on your behalf, and know that He does not want you to settle for less. God has more than average for you, but you must give Him your heart and put Him first. In doing this, keep these things in mind: wait for God to send you the right person, and keep your standards high; tell potential love interests, "No FWBs!"; and, in your waiting, God will bless you with the best, or, should I say, that "Summertime Fine" best! The next chapter illustrates what "Summertime Fine" should be.

CHAPTER 3

Summertime Fine

Everyone has a different perspective concerning what is attractive, though physical beauty is not always the determining factor for what we consider to be beautiful. It is human nature to look and notice how physically attractive someone is. The Bible relays several stories about how aesthetic beauty played a major role in relationships. King David, for instance, saw the beauty of Bathsheba and that enticed him to go after her. He was so taken by her beauty that he just had to have her. Today, she would have been considered "summertime fine."

"Summertime fine" is a colloquial term that some people use to express their pleasure with someone's looks. People equate this term with beauty—like when a man tells a beautiful woman that she is "summertime fine." Beauty—whether seen in the way a person carries himself/herself or in his/her physical features—is what initially attracts people to each other. God uses beauty many times to get a message across, or to fulfill a purpose. God knows what will attract you to bring you to a specific point in life. Beauty is mentioned in the Bible frequently. In Scripture, Absalom, one of David's sons, was described as a very attractive man; however, he revolted against the house of David and tried to take over the kingdom. A similar situation happened in heaven. When God created Lucifer, He gave him beauty, wisdom, and talent. But Lucifer wanted to take over the kingdom of God, and he wanted people to worship him as God. These examples show how beauty, talent, and wisdom were used the wrong way.

God created us all for His glory. God made you in His image (which is beauty), so give the glory to God, and don't let your beauty go to your head. You should not allow people's beauty to make you succumb to lust. Take the time to get to know a person to be able to see if he/she is a good fit for you. Plus, once you get to know a person for who he or she really is, you may realize that he or she is not as "summertime fine" on the inside as you originally thought. Also, you may become more attracted to a person once you get to know more about that person, and realize that beauty is deeper than physical features. You may meet someone that you may not be that attracted to physically, but once you get to know him/her the attraction changes. The person God has for you may not be what you think is "summertime fine" per the world's standards, but you must trust God to know what is best. Again, God knows what you need, and He will bless you with the best. And while God may give you everything you want physically in a person, too, you mustn't allow that to distract you from the important qualities.

Favour is deceitful, and beauty is vain: but a woman that feareth the LORD, she shall be praised.
(Proverbs 31:30)

Loving God must be the most important thing that we do. Love is the key to life, because life is all about love. A person who loves the Lord will be able to love you the right way, which means that he or she will pray for you. We can get so caught up in physical attraction that we forget about *agape* (unconditional) love. You can't experience agape love in a relationship based on lust and lies. As a matter of fact, to have unconditional love, you have to build a strong foundation. When God is the foundation of the relationship you will experience real agape love. Even when your "summertime fine" looks fade, your relationship will never fade.

Lust not after her beauty in thine heart; neither let her take thee with her eyelids. (Proverbs 6:25)

I know it is hard to not lust after someone's beauty, and it is hard not to let his/her beauty distract you. But looks can be deceiving and the heart is desperately wicked (see Jeremiah 17:9). As illustrated in the previous chapter, your lusting after someone you find aesthetically pleasing can lead you to destruction and it can destroy a relationship. King David and his son Solomon allowed lust to be one of their major downfalls, which ultimately destroyed their kingdoms. Had Solomon never married the strange women—those he thought were "summertime fine"—that God told him not to marry, he would have had a more prosperous reign as king.

Beauty is usually the number-one thing that attracts people; why do you think it is strategically used in advertising agencies? Most advertisers know that a good way to entice a man or woman to buy something is to use a sexy woman or man to sell it. This strategy has been used for decades, and the devil knows this, so he uses beauty and sex to deceive people. Furthermore, when people seem to be perfect and physically attractive and can easily seduce you with those good looks, this sends up a red flag. God will not send you someone who will seduce you and take your focus away from Him. God wants you to focus on Him. And when that happens, then

He will send you a significant other who is beautiful inside as well as out. You want someone who will bring that beauty out in you, someone who also has a special relationship with God; this will put your relationship on a godly level.

> **But the LORD said unto Samuel, Look not on his countenance, or on the height of his stature; because I have refused him: for the LORD seeth not as man seeth; for man looketh on the outward appearance, but the LORD looketh on the heart.**
> (1 Samuel 16:7)

When it comes to preparing for the right mate, it is important to pray and let God give you spiritual discernment about people in your life (He will do it, if you ask). People will eventually show you who they are, if you are observant. And you will notice that when people show you who they are, they will show you that they have a preference—and I believe that God can use your preference regarding attraction for your good. God will use things to get your attention. For example, you may be at the grocery store and see someone who is "summertime fine," so you approach the person and the two of you exchange numbers. Once you start dating, you get to know the person, and that is the first step to prepare for marriage.

God can use things to get your attention, especially since He knows what your preferences are. Don't allow someone's appearance to intimidate you from getting to know the person inside—he or she may be what God wants for you. Past conversations I've had with male associates have again shown how many men are enticed yet slightly intimidated by a woman's appearance. This knowledge serves as proof of the importance of knowing a person and observing his/her actions.

It is also good to know a potential love interest's background because, many times, a person's track record gives you an idea of his/her future. The worst thing you could do is become emotionally attached to someone and not know where he or she is going in life. As an example, someone who never finishes anything is usually going to lead a life of procrastination and not get things done. And while physical appearance can attract you, conversation is where true attraction begins. The more you get to know about someone, the more attractive he or she can become in your eyes, and vice versa. It is very important to ask questions in the beginning stages of dating, because that can save you from a lot of grief in the future. As a matter of fact, when you ask questions, expect and don't be afraid to get a detailed answer. Society has brainwashed us to stay away from conversation and go straight into sex, believing that all that matters is the physical attraction. Sex oftentimes clouds one's judgment and stops one from keeping the heart guarded. So, don't let someone seduce you into doing something you don't want to do because you think he/she is "summertime fine."

Having background information can help you better connect with a potential love interest, because (1) when issues arise you can better understand why the person is acting the way he or she is, and (2) the foundation you build with someone can help your relationship last longer. If the person you are dating is not opening up to you, that is a clear sign that he or she is not the right person for you. If you want someone just because he/she is "sexy," you may as well "Netflix and chill" (a colloquial phrase used for going to someone's home to watch movies and have sex) with that person, because you will not get far in that relationship otherwise. God wants you to be with someone who produces fruit through his/her purpose, whether he/she is "summertime fine" or not. When you get into a relationship with someone who produces positive fruit, you will produce great things together. You both can merge your individual goals together and help support each other. Relationships are meant for support, because it can sometimes be difficult to do things all by yourself. In relationships, we can help each other build the kingdom of God. Just like spreading the Gospel happens through conversation, it is through conversation that we learn to develop relationships with people.

Aside from our relationship with God, marriage is the most important earthly relationship, because the person you share your life with is supposed to be sanctioned by God, someone who can change your life for better or worse. Never jump into a marriage because of lust or infatuation. As a Christian, I believe in acknowledging God first, and asking Him, "Is this relationship for me?" From experience, I remember asking God if a particular person was for me, and within that same week He showed me what I needed to know. If you want God to show you if someone is for you, all you have to do is ask.

Ask, and it shall be given you; seek, and ye shall find; knock, and it shall be opened unto you.
(Matthew 7:7)

God wants you to ask, because when you ask you are acknowledging Him. Every time you talk to God and read His Word, you are building a relationship with Him. Your relationship with God is what matters the most, because you can trust and depend on Him. God will lead you in the right direction and you will meet the right people along the way. When you ask, be specific and honest with God. There is nothing wrong with being specific; God wants you to be bold enough to come to Him. When you're praying for specific things, it shows God how much faith you have to depend on Him, and He will give you what you desire, if it is in line with His will. And even if what you prayed for specifically isn't answered the way you thought it would be, there is a reason behind it. God knows the big picture and He wants to bless you, so don't be afraid to be specific and open with God. Even when it doesn't go as you have planned, God always has a better plan.

For I know the thoughts that I think toward you, saith the Lord, thoughts of peace, and not of evil, to give you an expected end. (Jeremiah 29:11)

God knows your expected end, so continue to trust Him and do good. When you are His child, He will save you from things that can destroy you—even if that means you don't get certain things that you think you want (like that "summertime fine" man or woman, ha ha). The blessings that are sent from God are always better. Sometimes what you pray for takes time to be revealed, because you must be prepared for it. For instance, many people pray for a spouse, and they expect God to send that person instantly. However, they have to be prepared and groomed for a spouse. When you're a child of God, He will prepare you for things before He gives them to you. If He gave you a spouse before the right time, you would mess things up, and it could hinder your relationship with Him. God wants your heart and complete focus to be on Him and the purpose that He has for you. Once you're prepared, and He knows that you're ready, your "summertime-fine bae" will cross your path.

The "summertime-fine" bae God has for you is already predestined, but it is your choice whether to follow the path that God has for you. God gave us free will, so the decisions you make are up to you. It is your choice whether you want to settle for less or wait on the spouse God has for you. Don't allow age, loneliness, or peer pressure to cause you to miss out on your blessing. If you wait, you will get what is best for you, and you won't have sorrow throughout your relationship; what you will have is agape love, which comes from God, and when God sends you a spouse, agape love is the foundation of the relationship.

Relationships that are not built on love don't last long. God has to be first. Plus, when you are waiting, you are being primped and prepared for what's to come. In the Bible, Esther had to wait for a while to meet with the king, because she had to be groomed and "summertime fine." You can't expect to have a king but not be prepared to be a queen. Esther knew her purpose, and knew that the king was the man God had set for her to help her save her people. Through her marriage, she fulfilled the purpose of saving the Jews from persecution. Waiting has a purpose, and is a great season to become the best you that God created you to be. If you are in the waiting season right now, say, "THANK YOU, LORD!" Keep waiting for your "summertime-fine" bae! Remember that the process of waiting doesn't hurt—it heals and prepares!

When God sends you a mate, continue to do what you did in the beginning; never take your spouse for granted. When looks fade, keep the spark between each other, and don't allow others to get in the middle. Don't allow physical appearance to link you to someone who is not meant for you. In other words, don't get married to someone because of how "summertime fine" the person is. Marry someone because of how he/she treats you through the thick-and-thin times, and build a godly friendship. Furthermore, build trust with that person before the two of you wed. Looks are not as important as intellect, trustworthiness, and morals. When you can have an intellectual and spiritual conversation with that person, that should seal the deal, because you will have great discernment and know you're on the right path.

Relationships only work when you converse and come to an understanding with one another. God wants you to be equally yoked to your spouse for that reason, because the relationship will be even harder to navigate with someone who is not on the same level as you. Relationships can be difficult, but even through the difficult moments you can handle things better when you're with someone who understands you. Overall, God wants the best spouse for you, but it is your choice to wait on God. And, always remember that waiting does not mean that you are not doing anything; instead, you are preparing—looking for the right person who is in accordance with God's Word, not the wrong person that the world portrays as right. To attract the right person, you must make sure that you are seeking God first. Again, when you seek God first, everything else will come when it's supposed to. Keep praying and actively waiting, and your "summertime fine" mate will come and bring that "old-school love" feeling into your life.

My parents, Drs. Louis and Betty Wade, in the 1980s

CHAPTER 4

Old-school Love

"Old-school love" is a term people use when they talk about how love used to be back in the day. Relationships from our grandparents' and parents' eras were different from what they are in our millennial era. Laws were different then, and the way people carried themselves was different. Today, people wait longer to get married, and love is just another four-letter word. There weren't as many single-parent homes then as there are now, and family dynamics were much different. Love, whether past, present, or future, still has the same meaning, but the actions behind the concept are different. Today, people are so consumed with social media fame, money, and beauty that they forsake the moral dynamics of love and family. So many people compete against one another and don't take the time to live their own lives. Back in our parents' and grandparents' times, all they had were each other, and they weren't caught up in societal games. They had a different perspective on love and relationships.

I recently interviewed my (maternal) grandmother, who at the time was seventy-eight years old. She was married to my grandfather for thirty-eight years until his death. They got married in the 1950s, at a time when people truly believed in "till death do us part." My grandparents stayed together through thick and thin, and they had six beautiful children. Please read the following questions I asked my grandmother about love and marriage:

1. **How did your generation view marriage?**

   My generation viewed marriage as being married forever; once you got married you were dedicated to your husband and children, and having everything perfect for them as a mother. We also believed in marriage till death do us part, no divorce.

2. **Why did you get married?**

   Well, I got married because we were taught to get married and live with our husband until till death do us part, and every girl in our day wanted to get married.

3. **What attracted you to my grandfather?**

   Well, he was a person that always stood by his word; if he said he was going to do something, he did it.

4. **How did you meet my grandfather?**

   I met your grandfather at my aunt's house for my grandfather's wake, before my grandfather's funeral.

My grandmother's generation was raised to believe in marriage; they did not believe in divorce, or living together before marriage. My grandmother was eighteen when she married my grandfather and stayed faithful to him until he died. Even when my grandfather was sick she took care of him; she never left his side. Marriages today barely last for five years, because people don't believe in commitment. It is sad to see people give up so quickly on marriage and not work through things. As a society, we should learn how to commit and stay together like our parents and grandparents did. We should learn how to have that "old-school love."

I also interviewed my mother and father about their marriage. They have been married for thirty-seven years and were blessed to raise me, their only child.

Please read the following questions I asked my mother:

1. **How did your generation view marriage?**

   My generation views marriage as sacred (holy). Also, marriage is supposed to be between a man and a woman, until death do us part.

2. **What are the keys to a long-lasting marriage?**

   Love is the first key to a long-lasting marriage, and allowing your husband to be the head of the house. Another key is communication; even through disagreements you must communicate with one another. Marriage is symbolic to Christ and the church, so it is important to love one another as Christ loves the church. Last, but not least, being affectionate toward each other is an important key to marriage.

3. **Why did you get married?**

   I got married because I was truly in love and [he] showered me with gifts all the time. Above all, he treated me like a queen, and he was very caring and the type of man I dreamed of. He has blessed me as a wife to help me grow in certain areas of my life.

4. **What advice would you give to newlyweds?**

   Stay close to each other and be affectionate toward one another. Don't resist your spouse's touch ever in a marriage, and always do things together. Also, learn how to listen to one another, and let nothing separate you.

5. **What attracted you to my father?**

   He was very consistent; he found me at a bus stop and kept pursuing me.

> **Husbands, love your wives, even as Christ also loved the church, and gave himself for it.** (Ephesians 5:25)

Now read the following questions I asked my father:

1. **How did your generation view marriage?**

   We viewed marriage as something sacred between a man and woman, and we believed in being married before having children.

2. **What are the keys to a long-lasting marriage?**

   The keys to a long-lasting marriage are trust, respect, honor, and love.

3. **As a man, what do you believe your role is in a marriage?**

   My role as a man is to lead my family to Christ and be the head of my house, and to make good decisions [in order] for my family to prosper. To be loving to my wife and child.

4. **Why did you get married?**

   I got married because I wanted to have a companion until the day I die, and to raise a family and carry on my name.

5. **What advice would you give to newlyweds?**

   The first advice I would give is to continue to date each other, and love one another.

6. **What attracted you to my mother?**

   I thought she was very attractive, and I liked her personality and the way she carried herself.

My parents, like many others from their generation, believe in the biblical principles of marriage. When they said "I do," they kept their vows and did not forsake their spouse. Marriage is a covenant, and we are supposed to keep that covenant sacred (holy) as with Christ and the church. We need to restore the morals and values of true love and relationships—not to mention that there needs to be standards placed on relationships, and we need to be clear with one another about those standards. The reason why so many people break up or divorce is because there was a lack of communication in the beginning, and lust was the only reason for why they dated each other. Marriage and relationships are work, and the foundation should always be built on biblical principles. Moreover, a marriage that lacks God is already condemned from the beginning. God is the glue to your relationship, and He is the only one that can keep the spark alive in your marriage. Even in the difficult times in your marriage you will get through them, and become closer, because of God. True love is Christ Jesus, and when you have a Christian background and a daily relationship with God, anything is possible. Power is even more evident when you are married to someone who is on the same spiritual level that you're on. So, whatever you go through in a marriage with your God-ordained spouse, you will conquer it.

God ordained marriage for a purpose. Marriage is something beautiful and can be a wonderful part of your life. As a married couple, you are supposed to use your marriage as a ministry and a positive example to the world. Yet, today there are so many negative examples of marriage which can deter people away from wanting to be married. Many people perceive marriage to be stressful, unhappy, boring, and repetitious. However, when I observe my parents' marriage, it isn't like that. Yes, marriage is work, but it can be adventurous and exciting, too. Plus, when you have a mutual goal and you help one another, marriage can be a blessing, because you make each other better. It is a blessing when you have someone you can depend on and trust. That is why it is good to wait on the right person and build on love while you are dating.

My parents are a great example of two godly people staying married, and doing the work of God. Their marriage of thirty-seven years is a testimony in itself—because today most people don't make it to ten years before they are divorced. It takes discipline and patience to be married to the same person for many years. We need to get back that old-school love, and learn how to stay committed. Loving someone outside of yourself is good for your health, and when you grow old with someone both of you will still be young at heart. I believe that companionship helps human beings live longer.

Love is the most important aspect of life, and it gives people the motivation to continue to be positive throughout life. Without love, you can't function to your highest ability. Love should be grounded in Christ, and He should be the perennial source of your life. When you love Christ, you become more complete and whole as an individual. The love of Christ in you will attract the right person, with whom you will develop a real, unconditional love. As committed couples have taught us, marriage is a bond that should never be broken, and we must learn to forgive and continue to love one other. The "old school" type of love should never die; we should always be willing to truly commit to the person that God sends to us.

As stated before, it's as though society today views love as a game and a way to get laid. Even the youth seem to believe that sex equates to love, and that they have to be sexual in order to be on the dating scene. But sex and love are two different things. So many teens go through horrible relationships filled with abuse because they were not taught to know the difference between love and sex. Then those teens become adults who bear the scars of the mistakes they made in their youth, which causes a lot of grief in their adult relationships. This is why it is important that we teach our youth about love, marriage, and sex. They are wanting this insight so badly that they are out with friends experimenting, because they are too afraid to have a conversation with an adult. And what makes it worse is that some adults can't even give them good advice, because they are not being good examples themselves.

If we could take the time to explain how being sexually active with the wrong person can have negative physical and mental ramifications, they would understand that sex and love are different. Teens who don't have the right examples of love and commitment in their lives are prone to experience abusive relationships, sexually transmitted diseases, abortions, and pregnancies. After all, as human beings, we have sexual desires. However, it is our job to teach the next generation about morals and values regarding sex and marriage. For instance, there is a reason why sex is only meant for marriage—for one thing, it saves you from a lot of grief. God loves us so much that He warns of certain things to prevent us from getting hurt. He wants us to have the best, and to be the best persons He created us to be.

Your giving yourself to people so easily can cause you to face many demonic forces that you don't have to face if you stay disciplined. You can't dishonor God and expect to reap the blessings He has for you. Yes, we all make mistakes, but we have to learn from them, realizing that God wants us to be blessed! Why not try things God's way and change how you date people? Maybe if you change the way you date, you will view things quite differently from the way you viewed things before. Plus, without sex being in the equation, you will have better discernment about the person you're dating. You want to have a long-lasting relationship, and that can only happen by knowing and understanding each other. Love develops even more over time once you know each other.

The older generation believed in love and commitment. Men and women respected each other more as compared to now. Women carried themselves differently, and weren't as easy going in their modesty. Men during those times were more committed and were willing to wait for the woman they wanted. Yet, even though things have changed with our society and how we view relationships, one thing that won't change is humanity's desire to be loved. Our society is so into social media and TV that we have begun to live our lives in accord with the people we see on TV or Facebook—but those people are probably not living the way we think they are, and they're probably not happy. We live in a world where we compare and compete so much that we forget to live and enjoy life like our parents and grandparents did. When they dated, they didn't have social media to broadcast everything; they spent quality time together and lived in the moment. We need to get back to learning how to spend quality time with one another, and not be so quick to post everything about our dating life and our marriage life on social media.

Incidentally, relationships on social media can be a facade that people use for multiple reasons, which can cause other people to want relationships for the wrong reasons. Social media can entice people to want something because "everyone else has it." You have to assess what your motives really are, why you want a relationship, and if you're even ready for that commitment. Plus, everyone goes through different seasons in his/her life, and the season you are experiencing now may be one where you are to wait and be still. God has a time for everything, including sending you a spouse. Don't let social media or TV control your life. God should be the Director of your life, and He knows what you need and want. He works things out according to His time and His will.

What if He doesn't send you a spouse—would you still love Him and not be consumed with the things of the world? God wants you to be patient and trust Him. There is nothing too hard for God; He will give you your heart's desire at the right divine time. I've witnessed so many beautiful love stories (including my parents'), and how they knew from the beginning that they were meant to be for each other. They respected each other, and believed in the old-school way. The old-school way was for the man to court the woman and then ask her to marry him, before they lived together and had kids. Back then, people had more standards and respect for one another. It's so rare to see many couples like that anymore, and it's sad because, deep down inside, people aren't happy. Family dynamics have changed, and that has caused a lot of pain for the next generation. We have to get back to love, and what it really means to love someone. Single-parent households are growing more and more every day, and kids see their parents doing things that are disgraceful.

Fathers aren't present like they used to be, and it is affecting the children, because they are missing an important person in the home. Men play a vital role in the household, because God created them to be protectors and providers for the family. Women cannot fill the role of a man, no matter how hard they try. Men are an important part of the family.

For the husband is the head of the wife, even as Christ is the head of the church: and he is the saviour of the body. (Ephesians 5:23)

Old-school love, like the love my parents share, will always be around. As a society, we have to let love come naturally, and let God work through us. Standards must be put back into place, and we must abound in them and not let people persuade us into lowering our standards. Love is the key to living a successful and full life. We must get back to that old-school love, and stop playing so many games and hurting each other. The next generation needs a good example, and it is up to us to show them one.

Let your light so shine before men, that they may see your good works, and glorify your Father which is in heaven. (Matthew 5:16)

CHAPTER 5

You're the One

    The Bible is filled with many love stories, and one of the stories that I examine in this chapter is the one illustrating Jacob's love for Rachel. When a man loves a woman, and knows that she is the one for him, there is nothing he will not do to get and keep her. Jacob was in love with Rachel from the very first moment he laid eyes on her. He made sure he spoke with her father about marriage. During biblical times, it was customary for the man to first speak to the woman's father about marriage before he even courted her. Men had to get the father's approval, and in Jacob's case he had to work seven years before he could marry Rachel. Jacob worked hard for seven years to marry Rachel, and when his seven years came to an end, Rachel's father, Laban, gave him Leah, his other daughter, instead. Laban gave the oldest daughter, Leah, to Jacob in marriage first, because of the culture's tradition. Laban had tricked Jacob, and Jacob was furious, because his heart was set for Rachel, and he had waited seven years to have her. Then, Laban made another deal with Jacob; he told Jacob that he could agree to work for him another seven years and then he could marry Rachel. So, since Jacob agreed to work for Laban an additional seven years, Laban kept his promise to let Jacob marry Rachel.

This story shows how much Jacob truly loved Rachel, and how he labored for years just to be with her. Jacob did everything it took to get the woman of his dreams, and loved her until the day he died. That is real love, and it is rare to see someone go to that extent to be with the one he/she loves. Jacob made up his mind that she was the one. He saw the value in Rachel, and respected her enough to work hard to get her. A good man will do everything it takes to be with the woman he loves. He will not lead her astray or disrespect her, but, instead, will wait for her and put in work to get and keep her. Jacob waited for his love, and didn't let anything or anyone stop him. He could have easily given up and left Laban's house, but his heart was set on Rachel.

As I mentioned in chapter 3, another love story is the story of Esther and King Xerxes. Out of all the women the king met, Esther was the only one that won his heart. It was already destined for her to be the queen for a reason, just as it was destined for Jacob to have Rachel. Those stories can relate to how things are today, and how God already has everything orchestrated in one's life. The Rachel or king you want will come in God's time, but you have to wait and prepare yourself for it. Esther waited a year before she met the king, and during that year she had to prepare her body and mind. The delay she experienced, as with Jacob, was put in place in order for future events to come to pass. In your waiting period, God is setting the stage for future events, and you are being prepared and pruned to rise to the next level.

But they that wait upon the LORD **shall renew their strength; they shall mount up with wings as eagles; they shall run, and not be weary; and they shall walk, and not faint.** (Isaiah 40:31)

Wait on your mate, and while you are waiting prepare yourself for that person. Even when you receive the blessing don't stop working for it, because marriage is a constant commitment you work on. As a matter of fact, God has the one predestined for your life, and you will know when you meet that person. On another note, you can tell whether someone is sent by God or by the enemy. A person that is sent by God will wait on you and honor you. If you're dating a person who just wants sex, and then, after the second date, he figures out that he is not going to "hit it" quickly, it is only a matter of time before the person will disappear. That is a good thing, because you don't want someone who has a lustful spirit. When God sends you someone that person will be filled with the Holy Spirit, and he/she will not lead you in the wrong direction. And to the women waiting on "the one," remember that when you settle down with a man you are making the choice to be with the man who will be leading your family, so you must choose wisely. And to the men, you have to remember that marriage is important, because you are choosing the woman to share your life with, and to have children with. I always think of this when dating: *If you can't see yourself having a child with someone, don't marry the person.*

Settling down with the wrong person can create a generation of children that aren't what God promised. There is a prime of example of this in the Bible. Abraham and Sarah didn't believe that they were going to have a son because of their ages, yet God promised them Isaac. Prior to this, like many of us have experienced, Abraham grew impatient and made the mistake of bringing forth Ishmael. He did not believe that Isaac, the one promised by God, was coming. Although they were past their prime childbearing ages, God still blessed them with Isaac, who produced many nations.

This story serves to let us know that we must sit back and let God do His perfect work. His promises always have several blessings attached—but we have to wait on *Him*. Furthermore, I believe that sometimes God will show us the person we're supposed to be with before we even meet him or her. If God has shown you the one then it may be years before you two meet—but true love waits. Sometimes, God will show you certain aspects of your future so that you will stay on the right path, but you have to believe and trust Him. I know that some things that God shows us may seem farfetched—like when He told Noah to build an ark—but it all has a purpose. The person you marry is for a purpose, and if you wait on the right one, then God will bless the union.

The blessing of the Lord, it maketh rich, and he addeth no sorrow with it. (Proverbs 10:22)

When preparing for a mate, the most important relationship to have is a true relationship with God. The one we must fall in love with first is Jesus; He is the one we should search for, and He is the only one who can lead and direct our paths. Once you come to the realization that Christ is THE ONE, you will be able to choose your mate carefully. When the love of Christ dwells in you, others that have that same love will be attracted to you. God wants us to be in love with Him to the point of surrendering our lives to Him. He knows what we need and what we want. In the eyes of God, marriage is beautiful because it glorifies Him. However, God will not give us something that we idolize more than Him. We must keep our eyes on Jesus, and then everything else will come in the divine time that God has set.

Something else to consider is the fact that in the interim of waiting on God to show you who He has for you, being single is a beautiful part of life, because you're becoming more and more like Christ. Single people who are celibate or virgins are learning how to be disciplined and put down their lustful desires. When you can put down your flesh, stay committed to God, and wait for His blessing, there is nothing that God will withhold from you. I believe that certain things you do as a single person may set the stage for those same things to occur in your marriage. For example, I believe that if you always have multiple sex partners as a single person, then when you are married similar things could occur. A person's track record doesn't lie—if you can't handle something small, then chances are you can't handle something big. Also, how you prepare yourself while you're single will make a big difference in your married life—it's like a warm-up before the game.

And in that same vein of conducting a warm-up, I believe that when you're single, it is okay to write down the qualities you want in a mate. You should have deal breakers and know what signs to look out for when you are dating someone. God always gives signs in order to show you whether someone is meant for you or not. I believe that the Holy Spirit will give you discernment about someone instantly, if you just pay attention. The right person will take his time with you, and be open to waiting on sex. He will court you and take the initiative to pray with you and for you. For the women preparing for "the one," you will know if a man is true if he is open and wants to commit to courting you without sex being on the table. If a man can wait on you sexually, that is a good sign. A real man of God is patient, and his Christian walk will speak for itself. For men looking for "the one," you will know this by how she carries herself and her Christian walk. You will know by the fruit she produces, and if she maintains a good reputation.

To attract the right person, you have to make sure that you yourself meet the expectations and qualities you want in someone. You can't ask for a man who is celibate and reads his Bible every day but you aren't doing the same. The saying "you attract what you are" is true, because men who are celibate aren't going to date a woman who wants sex on the first date. Plus, people can tell from a mile away whether you are a Christian by the way you carry yourself;

that alone will stop certain people from approaching you. It is a good thing when certain people will not approach you, because they aren't on the same level as you. You want to attract people that have the same qualities as you. If you don't have the same qualities as the person you want, you should find ways to better yourself. If you want a spouse that isn't so easily drawn in by lustful things, yet you still watch porn, that needs to change. Furthermore, if you want someone who is healthy, yet you still eat out every day, that needs to change. Become the person you want, and eventually the right person will be attracted to you. And I understand that it is hard to live in a society that portrays relationships, sex, and marriage as something that isn't that serious—but to God, these are serious matters.

    Marriage is very important to God, and it is a covenant that two people take a vow to honor. Still, the time that God is giving you to be single is a blessing, because when you're single, you don't have to be responsible for taking care of a spouse, or compromising your life for someone else. God is giving you time as a single person to find your purpose and work in your purpose. When you're married or in a relationship it is harder to focus on what you're wanting to accomplish, because you are committed to someone else whom you have to consider when making decisions. When you're single, you can use that time to accomplish a lot and to prepare a good life for yourself and your future spouse. Single time does not have to be lonely time; instead, it should be busy time. You should be so busy that you forget you don't have a mate. Be busy doing God's work and fulfilling the purpose He gave you—that's the most important part of life.

    When you're walking in your purpose, you will attract the right person. Just keep working. God wants you to walk into your purpose, and He wants you to be focused on Him. Don't allow desperation and loneliness to be the focus of your single time. Desperation can cause you to fall for the wrong person, and cause you to become obsessed with the idea of marriage. Consider how desperation is displayed a lot on social media by so many single women, to the point that it becomes the center of many of their posts. Singleness is no longer looked at as a gift anymore, but, instead, is looked at as a burden.

Preparing for the one takes time and requires patience. Even when you meet "the one," it takes time to build a foundation for marriage. Patience is the key to any relationship. When you're getting to know a person, and you realize he is the one, you still have to prepare for marriage with that person. Single time is when you prepare yourself, and when you date, that is the time you both prepare together for marriage. Meeting the right one, once you *become* the right one, is a great way to start a stable foundation. Also, seeking premarital counseling is another good step to take while you're dating. Nevertheless, the following scenarios are examples of different relationships with Scriptures as a reference. These examples are used to help those reading this book to understand the importance of marriage and relationships when it is done the way God intended.

Example 1

Tony is a single man who has a great career, has no kids, and is a Christian. However, Tony is a lady's man. He likes to date and keep his options open. Recently he went on a date with a woman that he met at a night club. The night of their first date, they had sex. The next morning, he awoke to a note that she wrote stating, "Last night was wonderful, thanks for the thrill." Tony called his friends to brag about his "wonderful" night and then continued with his day. However, after that night he felt a sense of emptiness—it was like something had zapped his energy. He didn't realize what he had opened himself up to on the night of the date. That following Sunday, he went to church and he met this beautiful woman that he had never seen at church before. When he noticed her, he couldn't help but approach her and ask her out on a date. So, they went out on a couple of dates, and things were going very well. On the third date, she told Tony that she was celibate, and Tony was astounded because he had never dated a woman like her. It made him think twice if he wanted to continue dating her, because he wasn't celibate, even though he knew it was the right thing to do before God. Yet, Tony was very attracted to this woman, and he continued to date her, and eventually wanted to marry her.

  One day at work, he could barely stand; he felt dizzy and hit the floor. His co-workers called the ambulance and he was rushed to the hospital. While at the hospital, he told the doctor that he hadn't been feeling well for the past week but thought it was just a virus going around at work. After they ran tests, the doctor asked him about his sex life, and Tony thought that was a strange thing for the doctor to ask. When the tests came back, the doctor told Tony that he was HIV positive, and all Tony could think about was all the different women he had slept with over the years. He felt as if he lost everything, because he finally found a woman that he really cared for.

  The moral of this story is to wait for the right person, and to stop having sexual relations with multiple people. If Tony would have been more disciplined and not so quick to give in to having sex with every woman he met, he would have never caught HIV. Most importantly, he would have been able to settle down with the right woman. Whenever you have multiple sex partners you are exposing yourself to diseases, and that can have a big impact on your future. It really is important to wait, because it will save you from a lot of pain. Sex before marriage is a sin, and it is more addictive than any drug, because you're exchanging spirits and that leads to soul ties.

And if a man entice a maid that is not betrothed, and lie with her, he shall surely endow her to be his wife. (Exodus 22:16)

Flee fornication. Every sin that a man doeth is without the body; but he that committeth fornication sinneth against his own body. (1 Corinthians 6:18)

Example 2

Patrick was in his second year of college and was the star player of his basketball team. His coach believed that he would be the next superstar out of their university to become a pro basketball player. Patrick always had women chasing after him, and he knew he could have anyone he wanted. However, Patrick began practicing celibacy the summer before his sophomore year, after he and his girlfriend broke up. He started reading his Bible more every day and prayed to God for wisdom and success. When he surrendered his life to Christ, that is when he became better on the court and did better in his classes. He played so well that after his junior year, he was the number-one draft pick, and he played very well in the professional league. Patrick was so focused and really loved Christ; he committed to living his life for Christ. Some of the women he dated were not okay with his being celibate. He didn't want to settle for just anyone, so he continued to wait for his future wife. After two years of being in the league and making a good name for himself, he met someone that he knew was a Godsend. She was very successful, came from a great family, and believed in celibacy. They became best friends and did a lot of great things together in the community. After eight months of dating, Patrick could not wait any longer to propose to her. About six months later they both said "I do," and the "angels in heaven were rejoicing." Their marriage was blessed.

This example shows how God will bless you above and beyond what you could even ask for, if you live right. No one is perfect, and we all make mistakes; however, we must be willing to follow Christ and abide by His Word. God can't bless mess, so if you want to live successfully in Christ, and receive every blessing He has for you, then there must be some changes made in your life.

    I pray that this book will help anyone who is single or knows someone who is single. I want people to realize that being single is a blessing, because God is giving you time to become a better person. Looking for Mr. Right or Mrs. Right is not going to do you any good if you're not the right person yourself. I reiterate that in order to attract what you want, you have to meet the requirements that you want your right mate to possess. When you're single, you have more time to build your career and focus more on your relationship with God. Be grateful to have time to develop and grow as an individual, and don't settle for having "friends with benefits" relationships. Don't allow loneliness to force you into a relationship that isn't God-driven. I know that celibacy is a hard thing for people, and that not lusting after a "summertime fine" person is hard to do, but it is better to do it God's way than the world's way. Waiting is a blessing, while settling is a mistake. You are worth waiting for, and if someone doesn't want to wait for you, then it is best to keep it moving. When God sends the right person into your life, you will know it, and sorrow will not be behind it. Yes, you will have some hard days together, but your marriage will last and nothing will be able to tear you apart—and it will be like that "old-school love."

    Nonetheless, while waiting for your spouse, you should prepare yourself and live a life of celibacy. In all honesty, living a life of celibacy before marriage will help you become disciplined and not succumb to lustful temptation. There will be times in a marriage when you may have to go without having sex with your spouse (for example, after a woman gives birth). So, if you can learn how to be disciplined in that area as a single person, it will help you when you're married. What you practice in your single life will sometimes affect your married life. So, as a single person, you must learn patience, and you must prepare yourself for your spouse.

In conclusion, remember that singleness is a blessing from God, so you should take advantage of it and take the time to grow closer to God! So, if you don't take anything else away from this book, remember this: "pray, and wait, while you're preparing for the right mate."

God Is All About Love

*It's all about love,
When God sent His Son,
Nothing more precious from heaven above.
Jesus is love and the chosen one,
He who died for our iniquities—
Lord and Savior, there is none like Thee.
This love is all you need,
No man, no woman can compare,
The pain He endured and had to bear
For us to become joint-heirs.
Remember it's all about love,
Love is God and God is love.*

—Tiffany Wade

"Wisdom can help you get things that money can't buy."

About the Author

Tiffany L. Wade was raised in Nashville, Tennessee, and currently resides in Atlanta, Georgia. The daughter of Drs. Louis and Betty Wade, she is a graduate of Middle Tennessee State University, with a Master's degree in Professional Studies, and a Bachelor's degree in Mass Communication.

She has produced radio shows on remotes for Cumulus Media for more than seven years; has been interviewed on Extra Entertainment News (while in college), and worked in production with Nashville's Channel 5 WTVF *Talk of the Town* in 2010 as an intern.

Wade has been blessed to experience both sides of the entertainment industry. In addition to her entertainment career, she founded and developed a Summer Youth program for Youth ages thirteen to eighteen, "Building Youth Partnerships," in 2012. She continues to serve as the CEO and Director of the program and has added a Youth Speak Out tour, which was started in 2015 in Nashville, Tennessee. Her goal is to empower and speak to youth around the world.

Moreover, Wade was nominated for Community Ambassador for the National Youth Activism Awards in Nashville, Tennessee, in 2015. She has been the recipient of many honorary awards. She has also been able to create events with her youth program, and be a part of several youth events and women events as the guest speaker around the community. Her goal is to use all her gifts to glorify God, and to bring people together.

In her private time, Wade enjoys cooking, writing, singing, songwriting, and spending time with her family. Her favorite Scripture verse is Romans 8:28.

www.ingramcontent.com/pod-product-compliance
Lightning Source LLC
Chambersburg PA
CBHW070551300426
44113CB00011B/1867